Niagara Falls

HISTORIC PHOTO ALBUM

PRESENTED BY THE NIAGARA GAZETTE

Acknowledgements

The Niagara Gazette would like to extend our sincere appreciation and gratitude to the following organizations and individuals. Without their invaluable assistance and photo contributions, this book would not have been possible.

Don Glynn

Audrey Perry

Sam Golden

Donald Loker

Niagara Gazette staff writers

Ray Wigle, Old Fort Niagara

Porter Historical Society

Niagara County Historical Society

Niagara Falls Public Library: Betty Babanoury, Director and Maureen Fennie, Manager Local History/Public Services

The numerous Niagara Falls area residents that generously contributed their photos and information

Copyright© 2000 • ISBN: 1-891395-49-1
Published by Pediment Publishing, a division of The Pediment Group, Inc. www.pediment.com

TABLE OF CONTENTS

Foreword

As the new century dawns, the city seeks to recapture the crowning image once emblazoned on the masthead of *The Niagara Falls Gazette: "King of Power, Queen of Beauty."*

This wide-ranging collection of photos — many contributed by local residents — offers a glimpse of our rich heritage, from the era of hydropower development and the industrial complex along Buffalo Avenue to the mom-and-pop stores that flourished before shopping malls and the numerous civic organizations that were such a vital part of the community fabric.

Although a mere random sampling, the photo album captures the way we were in the late 1800s and through most of the 20th Century. It provides us with sharp reminders of the awesome beauty of the falls and the gorge, the bridges which linked the Cataract Cities and their two nations, and Falls Street in its bustling days, when people could park diagonally and walk to a theater or restaurant.

We hope that as you browse through this collection, it will remind you of the dynamic forces that shaped our community. The plant workers whose skills helped us become the 'Electrochemical Capital of North America,' 'The Home of Shredded Wheat' and 'The Power City.'

The family-owned small businesses that were an integral part of the neighborhood. And the world-famous destination that made us a magic dateline in the media, a unique 'Honeymoon Capital.'

We also hope this book will renew your faith that a *new* NIAGARA is on the horizon.

THE FALLS

T he view from the base of the American Falls has changed dramaticlly over the decades.

Today, much of the sheer drop of the 180-foot waterfall is hidden by the massive Prospect Point rockiest in July 1954, when an estimated 185,000 tons of rock broke away from the face of the cliff.

A study was undertaken in 1969 (Page 14) to determine what remedial measures might be taken to prevent further rock slides. To complete that probe, a coffer dam was built at the eastern end of Goat Island, with all the water diverted over the Horseshoe Falls.

After the 18-month study by the U.S. Army Corps of Engineers, geologists and the International Joint Commission (IC), it was decided to let Nature take its course.

Tourists enjoying an outing at the American Falls. *Courtesy, Niagara Falls Public Library*

The American Falls at the Bridal Veil, 1890s. *Courtesy, Marlene Beazley*

The Falls, American and Horseshoe taken from Prospect Point, circa 1885.
Courtesy, Niagara Falls Public Library

The railway suspension bridge looking up the whirlpool rapids, at Niagara from the Canadian side. *Courtesy, Marlene Beazley*

Aerial view, American Falls, Luna Island, Luna Falls, Goat Island and Horseshoe Falls. *Courtesy, Niagara County Historical Society*

American Falls from
Goat Island, circa
1945. *Courtesy, Niagara
Falls Public Library*

Maid of Mist boat tours at the docks, 1930s. *Courtesy, Barbara Morcom*

American Falls from the Canadian side, 1920s. *Courtesy, Niagara Falls Public Library*

American Falls from Goat Island, 1890s. *Courtesy, Marlene Beazley*

Sightseers viewing the ice and snow. *Courtesy, Alice Smith Lasher*

Two people on Prospect Point viewing a very frozen American Falls. *Courtesy, Niagara County Historical Society*

Luna Island during the winter, American Falls in the background, Luna Falls in the foreground. *Courtesy, Niagara County Historical Society*

The American Falls, frozen to a dry situation. The Honeymoon Bridge is to the left. *Courtesy, Niagara County Historical Society*

The frozen falls. *Courtesy, Mark Johnston*

The Ice Palace, built on Prospect Park in Niagara Falls, 1890. *Courtesy, Niagara County Historical Society*

Ice flow on upper Niagara River, January 1938. *Courtesy, Jeff Merlin*

Ice flow destroyed the Honeymoon Bridge, 1938. *Courtesy, Jeff Merlin*

Frozen falls taken from Canadian side, circa 1930. *Courtesy, Rose Scarcelli*

Collapse of the Honeymoon Bridge, January 1938. *Courtesy, Mark Johnston*

DE-WATERING THE FALLS

Niagara Falls has long been world famous as a magnificent scenic wonder and bountiful source of power. With the passing of time the tremendous force of rushing water gradually cut back the crestlines of the Falls. The immediate results of the erosion were most evident at the American Falls where great volumes of fallen rock accumulated at the base of the Falls marring the spectacle of an uninterrupted view of water.

From July through December 1969, water that rushed down the American Channel and tumbled over the precipice was stopped. The purpose — to investigate the geologic conditions of rock strata of the American Falls.

American Falls, dewatered, 1969. *Courtesy, Niagara Falls Public Library*

American Falls, dewatered, 1969. *Courtesy, Niagara Falls Public Library*

THE DAREDEVILS

On September 7, 1827, hotel owners put several wild animals aboard a condemned Lake Erie schooner named "Michigan" and sent it plummeting over the Horseshoe Falls as advertised before a crowd of more than 10,000 people. Thus began 172 years of recorded history of men and women challenging the Niagara River and the Falls in the face of death for fame and fortune. They came willingly and gambled their very lives.

Balleni on his tightrope, late 1800s. *Courtesy, Niagara Falls Public Library*

Balleni had an act called "Couchone Leap," in which he dropped from his cable to the river at the end of a rubber line. As he released the rubber, it flew back to the cable and he fell into the river, where he was picked up by a small boat and taken to shore. This photo shows Signor Balleni making the Couchone Leap from his rope into the Niagara River, 1870s. *Courtesy, Niagara Falls Public Library*

Steve Peer, tight rope performance over the rapids, late 1800s. Peer, a Drummondville Ont. painter, helped to erect Signor Balleni's rope, and asked Balleni's permission to walk it. This was refused, but one day Peer picked up Balleni's balancing pole and struck out from Canada for the New York side, performing on the way over. He did well, and he walked at other times surreptitiously. This angered Balleni. One day when Peer was on the rope, Balleni was caught trying to cut the cable at the American end. Angry witnesses forced him to desist, he was driven away, and fled to Canada, where he was arrested, but released after which he disappeared, but not before "Billy" Goodfellow, a friend of Peer's, in Canada gave him a sound whipping.

Courtesy, Niagara Falls Public Library

Samuel Dixon crossing Niagara below the Great Cantilever Bridge, 1890s. *Courtesy, Niagara Falls Public Library*

Blondin carrying Henry N. Colcord on his shoulders, August 19, 1859.
Courtesy, Niagara Falls Public Library

Jean Francois Gravelet "The Great Blondin," wearing his many medals. He performed on his rope across the Niagara Gorge, summers of 1859 and 1860. *Courtesy, Niagara Falls Public Library*

Farini (William Hunt) walks his tightwire as "Biddy O'Flaherty," summer, 1860. *Courtesy, Niagara Falls Public Library*

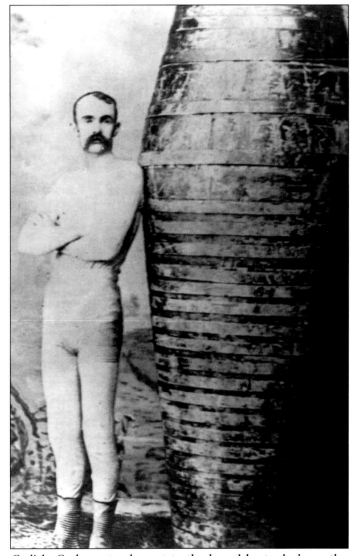

Carlisle Graham stands next to the barrel he took down the rapids, July 11, 1886. Graham was the first barrel stunter at the falls. *Courtesy, Niagara Falls Public Library*

Marla Spelterini was the only woman to tightrope across the Niagara River. She crossed in 1876 with peach baskets on her feet. The Niagara Falls Suspension Bridge is in the background. *Courtesy, Niagara County Historical Society*

Clifford Calverley during one of his crossings. *Courtesy, Niagara Falls Public Library*

Clifford Calverley during one of his 1893 crossings, balancing himself with the aid of a long pole. Weights and guide wires kept the 1300-foot cable taut.
Courtesy, Niagara Falls Public Library

Last walk across Niagara River, on a 5/8 inch wire, June 22, 1887. *Courtesy, Niagara Falls Public Library*

William Kendall, a Boston policeman, managed to paddle through the lower rapids in 1886, protected with only a life preserver. *Courtesy, Niagara Falls Public Library*

Mrs. Annie Edson Taylor, 43, became famous for going over the Falls in a barrel, October 24, 1901. At left, she poses with her cat and a reproduction of the barrel. Above, she is being helped across a walkway after her ride over the Falls. *Courtesy, Niagara Falls Public Library*

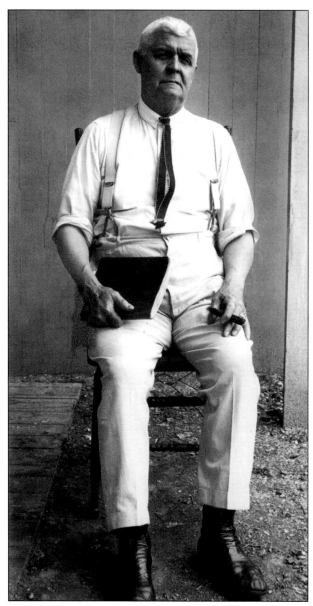

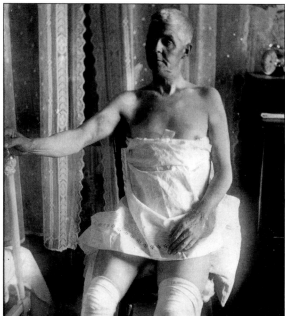

Bobby Leach went over the Horseshoe Falls in a barrel July 25, 1911. At left he is shown bandaged, indicating how badly he was bruised. Below, Bobby Leach and his barrel after his perilous trip over the Falls.

Courtesy, Niagara Falls Public Library

Lincoln Beachey flew his biplane under the Upper Steel Arch Bridge, June 27, 1911. *Courtesy, Niagara Falls Public Library*

Jean Lussier planned his trip over the Falls for several years and spent $7,000 in making preparations. The ball in which he made the trip was of steel frame, covered with 10-ply reinforced rubber, while he was held in place inside with pillows and belts. An estimated one-hundred thousand people came to watch his feat. *Courtesy, Niagara Falls Public Library*

Lussier, after his ride over the Falls, July 4, 1928. *Courtesy, Niagara Falls Public Library*

Jean Lussier posing for the camera after his ride over the Falls, July 4, 1928. *Courtesy, Niagara Falls Public Library*

William "Red" Hill sitting in his famous barrel in the Niagara River, circa 1920. *Courtesy, Niagara County Historical Society*

"Red" Hill Jr., in his rubber tube called the "thing" before he went over the Falls. Red Hill Jr. emulated his father and wanted to surpass him. Lacking funds to build a proper barrel, he settled for a contraption of inner tubes. He made the plunge on September 1, 1948 and died in a tangle of rubber tubes and netting. *Courtesy, Niagara County Historical Society*

William Kondrat, age 18, of Chatham, New Jersey, swam out from the old Maid of the Mist landing and was caught in the whirlpool rapids. He landed in the whirlpool on the Canadian side alive and made his way up the bank to the Aero car, where he was given an old pair of overalls. Kondrate was the first person known to have gone through the whirlpool rapids unaided by a life preserver, boat or barrel and come out alive. The owner of the restaurant in which Kondrat ate before going through the rapids heard about the experience and sang: "Eat my sandwiches, eat my pie; go through the rapids, but do not die." *Courtesy, Niagara Falls Public Library*

TRANSPORTATION

The bridges over Niagara have provided a key link in the development of tourism and commerce along the international border. Some of their names have changed over the years. The Rainbow Bridge, which was completed in the early 1940s, was the successor to the famous Honeymoon Bridge (also known as the Fallsview Bridge and the Upper Steel Arch Bridge) which was destroyed by an ice jam in the lower Niagara River in January 1938.

The Whirlpool Bridge, known to local residents as the Lower Bridge, was built in the 1890s. The Lewiston-Queenston Bridge, which opened in the early 1960s, links the I-190 (Niagara Expressway) with the Queen Elizabeth Way in Toronto.

Also, in this chapter, some railroads including the New York Central which brought countless visitors to Niagara, and The Cayuga, the steamship which carried thousands of passengers each season between Lewiston, N.Y., and Toronto. That service ended in the mid-1950s although there have been several unsuccessful attempts to revive it in recent years.

This automobile transported Dorothy Willick to Goat Island in 1936. *Courtesy, Barbara Willick*

Lower Suspension Bridge. *Courtesy, Niagara Falls Public Library*

Chinese Embassy riding over the river in a "basket" attached to the cables of the new Suspension Bridge, circa 1868. *Courtesy, Niagara Falls Public Library*

The Upper Suspension Bridge, 1880s. The bridge was built in 1868, wrecked in 1888, rebuilt in 1889 and moved to Lewiston when the Upper Steel Arch Bridge was built, 1897-98. *Courtesy, Niagara Falls Public Library*

Early view of the Upper Suspension Bridge. *Courtesy, Niagara County Historical Society*

These workers are building the Upper Suspension Bridge, 1880s. *Courtesy, Niagara Falls Public Library*

Early view of the Upper Suspension Bridge. *Courtesy, Niagara Falls Public Library*

The Whirpool Rapids Bridge in 1890 was a crowd-getting tourist attraction. Visitors from all over the world came to see the railway suspension bridge.

Courtesy, Niagara Falls Public Library

Crew and passengers pose in front of a New York Central train, early 1900s. *Courtesy, Niagara Falls Public Library*

Crowd gathers near the NYC train at the depot on Second Street - crossing of railroad and trolley car. The trolley car is at the signal tower. *Courtesy, Niagara Falls Public Library*

Railroad engine "Niagara," circa 1905. *Courtesy, Niagara Falls Public Library*

Niagara Junction Railroad engine being raised from Niagara River at the foot of Iroquois Street, Niagara Falls, where it had fallen in. *Courtesy, Niagara Falls Public Library*

Lasalle Rail office between Erie and New York Central tracks at Cayuga Drive and Buffalo Avenue, circa 1900. *Courtesy, Alice Smith Lasher*

One of the cars on the old ride along the Niagara Gorge-pre Niagara Gorge Railway tours.

New York Central train crew, June 12, 1901. Left to right: Robert Scouter, brakeman; George Scott, engineer; William Green, fireman; Burt Shank, James Walker, conductor; Joe Baker, brakeman. The train cost 35 cents between Niagara Falls and Buffalo. *Courtesy, Niagara Falls Public Library*

Gorge Trolley Line. *Courtesy, Barbara Willick*

A group of workers at the railroad office near 11th Street in the north end, circa 1920. *Courtesy, Audrey Perry*

Passenger Train Station in North end bordered by North Avenue and Grove, early 1950s. *Courtesy, Alfred Frosolone*

New York Central's freight house was the last structure to go in the railroad relocation project on Little Fourth Street, 1965. *Courtesy, Eugene Dickson*

Steamer Cayuga, Lewiston to Toronto, circa 1910. *Courtesy, Lewiston Historical Society*

Mr. and Mrs Eugene Kinsey take a spin in the "Niagara" automobile, designed and built by Eugene, circa 1903. *Courtesy, Niagara Falls Public Library*

Martin Donohue, city electrician, rides in this early automobile, 1916. *Courtesy, Niagara Falls Public Library*

A popular early form of transportation for children. Donald D. Krueger Sr., at left, grew up to own Krueger Pontiac in Niagara Falls. On the right is Robert Krueger, later owner of Krueger Chevrolet. *Courtesy, Kimberly Stotlemyer*

PUBLIC SERVICE

The people who serve the citizens are an integral part of any community.

Niagara Falls has always been fortunate with its dedicated public servants, especially the police officers and firefighters who continue to provide splendid service. In earlier days, before the Public Safety Building was built on Hyde Park Boulevard, the police and fire headquarters were side-by-side at Niagara and Second streets, a block now occupied by a parking ramp.

Firemen at the Cataract House fire, October 14, 1945. From left to right: Fred Hurst, Joseph Birmingham, Harold Chamberlain, Everett Giroux, Bill Clambrone, John Mallory (S.A.). *Courtesy, Ruth Paterniti*

Niagara fire department headquarters, at Niagara and Second streets, late 1800s. *Courtesy, Niagara Falls Public Library*

Hose Company No. 5, Niagara Falls, late 1800s. *Courtesy, Niagara Falls Public Library*

Niagara Falls Fire Department headquarters, late 1880s. *Courtesy, Audrey Perry*

Niagara Avenue fire department, Niagara Falls, 1900. *Courtesy, Niagara Falls Public Library*

10th Street fire department, Niagara Falls, circa 1910. *Courtesy, Niagara Falls Public Library*

LaSalle Town Hall, police station and jail, 1927. Presently Lasalle Library. The watertank in the background was taken down in 1928. *Courtesy, Roy Richardson*

Dedication of City Hall, Niagara Falls, May 1925. *Courtesy, Niagara Falls Public Library*

Captain John (Jack) Dietz retirement party. *Courtesy, Geraldine Biehl Tracey*

Motorcycle squad inspection, circa 1950. *Courtesy, Geraldine Biehl Tracey*

Captain Dietz makes a routine check-up of the motorcycle squad, circa 1950. *Courtesy, Geraldine Biebl Tracey*

Company E home from the War, 1919. *Courtesy, Audrey Perry*

This group of U.S. Marines from Niagara Falls relaxes for a few minutes on the Russell Islands in the Pacific during World War II, shortly after landing on Okinawa in April 1945. The fighting in that area was among the fiercest in the war. Japan formally surrendered later that year in a ceremony aboard the USS Missouri. Left to right, standing, Pvt. Angelo Conde, Pfc. Michael Colucci, Pvt. Patrick O'Sullivan, and Pvt. Joseph A. Forcucci. Kneeling, Pfc. Anthony Amantia, Pfc. Angelo Fracassi. Pvt. Silvio Sepielli and Pfc. Charles Sicurella. They were all members of the 5th Marines, 1st Division. *Courtesy, Don Glynn*

Old Fort Niagara, circa 1896. *Courtesy, Niagara Falls Public Library*

Officers' Quarters, Fort Niagara. *Courtesy, Office of Niagara County Historian*

Field Kit inspection, Fort Niagara. *Courtesy, Office of Niagara County Historian*

The "French Castle" at Old Fort Niagara, circa 1879, shows the result of decades of alterations by the U.S. Army. The pedestal on the roof held the Fort Niagara navigational light until the lens was transferred to the new lighthouse in 1871. *Courtesy, National Archives*

Aerial view of Hyde Park Stadium in 1934, showing the construction of the stage for the "Four Nation Celebration" to mark the restoration of Old Fort Niagara. *Courtesy, Old Fort Niagara Association*

STREET SCENES

From Main Street in the city's North End to Highland Avenue and Hyde Park Boulevard (originally Sugar Street), to Pine Avenue, the Buffalo Avenue industrial complex, and the South End, the streets are filled with stories.

Without a doubt, however, the most famous address is (Old) Falls Street, now a pedestrian mall between the Lackey Plaza and the entrance to the state park.

The city now faces the challenge of reviving Falls Street, to make it as bustling for tourists and local residents as it was in the first half of the 20th Century.

A view of Falls Street, circa 1927. A banner high above the street promotes Memorial Hospital's 1927 Building Fund Campaign. *Courtesy, Memorial Medical Center Foundation*

Main Street, early 1900s. *Courtesy, Barbara Willick*

In the early 1900s, the city market was in the northern end of the city on Main Street and Linwood Avenue. Fred Dean, whose barn can be seen on the left, was market clerk. At the right is the old Market Hotel. The police officer in the foreground is Michael Hogan, with Washington Frazer and Fred Dean standing next to him. *Courtesy, Francis Eames*

View of Center Street, Lewiston, circa 1850. *Courtesy, Lewiston Historical Society*

Center Street, Lewiston, 1880. *Courtesy, Lewiston Historical Society*

City Market on Pine Avenue, late 1800s. *Courtesy, Niagara Falls Public Library*

Falls Street with trolley tracks, early 1900s. *Courtesy, Barbara Willick*

Main Street south of Michigan Avenue in front of Marine Trust Company.
Courtesy, Cliff Collins

Falls Street and Post Office looking east, Niagara Falls, circa 1900. *Courtesy, Audrey Perry*

Falls Street looking west from Third, 1931. *Courtesy, Andrew and Virginia Ligammari*

Falls Street, looking west from Second Street, Niagara Falls. circa 1920. *Courtesy, Niagara County Historical Society*

Basil's LaSalle Theater, LaSalle Soda Shop, Loblaw's Grocery Store, Buffalo Avenue at 76th Street, 1938. The movies playing were: "Kidnapped" and "He Couldn't Say No." *Courtesy, Roy Richardson*

Main Street and Portage Road, 1947, later the "Y" Coffee Shop. *Courtesy, Cliff Collins*

Shea's Bellevue Theatre across from Jenss Department Store, North Main Street, 1947. *Courtesy, Cliff Collins*

Highland Avenue Bridge, removed early 70s. Photo, circa 1955. *Courtesy, Alfred Frosolone*

Highland Avenue looking south, early 1950s. *Courtesy, Alfred Frosolone*

Eugene and Ann Dickson walking on Falls Street, 1959. *Courtesy, Eugene Dickson*

Gluck building fire, Falls Street west of Third Street, 1959. *Courtesy, Mark Johnston*

Gluck building fire, 1959. *Courtesy Mark Johnston*

The foot of Falls Street, 1960. *Courtesy, Barbara Willick*

Cataract Theater on Falls Street, looking east, circa 1967. *Courtesy, Niagara Falls Public Library*

Falls Street, looking east from Prospect Street, 1963. *Courtesy, Angelo Ciraolo*

Falls Street at night in the 1960s.

SOCIETY

A look at Niagara's community organizations, its churches and civic groups. St. Mary of the Cataract Church, Fourth Street, adjacent to the Convention and Civic Center, traces its roots to the 1840s, the oldest Roman Catholic Church in the county.

In Youngstown, the First Presbyterian Church, Main Street, was built in 1837.

Part of the vanishing scene also is found in these pages. The First Evangelical Church, Cleveland Avenue and 16th Street, was at one time the home of the Niagara Falls Little Theater.

Scholarship winners at Holy Trinity Church, Father Cyman, Chester Tubinis, Theresa Maljchrzak and Father Glowacki of St. Stanislaus Church ceremony presenting scholarships to two girls and two boys of the parish by the Polish Central Council. *Courtesy Echo Club*

St. John's Episcopal Church at Main and Chestnut streets, Youngstown. The congregation was officially organized in April of 1868. The corner stone for this building was laid May 16, 1878. *Courtesy, Town of Porter Historical Society*

Laying the cornerstone, St. Paul's Methodist Episcopal Church. *Courtesy, Niagara Falls Public Library*

First Evangelical Church, Cleveland and 16th. *Courtesy, Niagara Falls Public Library*

Laying the cornerstone, St George's Church, circa 1927. *Courtesy, Niagara Falls Public Library*

St. Mary of the Cataract Church, 4th Street, early 1900s.

First Presbyterian Church in Youngstown. This building was erected in 1837 at a cost of $2,600. *Courtesy, Town of Porter Historical Society*

"Beveronia" student fraternity of Latvia, Niagara Falls, 1959. *Courtesy, Paul D. Kaczmarzyk*

St. Paul Evangelical Lutheran Church, Cleveland and 18th. *Courtesy, Niagara Falls Public Library*

Echo Club concert at Hotel Niagara, 1948-1949. *Courtesy, Jean Dojka*

Wedding in 1921. Standing left to right, Stephanie Szczes, Charles Chrzanowski, Sigmund Dojka, the groom, Raymond Dojka, Ben Kaszyca, Ida Szczes. Sitting, Felixa Pasek, the bride, and Mary Penczek.

Dupont Women's banquet, 1957.

This unidentified photo taken by a local photographer in Niagara Falls, appears to be a pretend wedding at a school. *Courtesy, Jim and Jody Gray*

This group poses at a party at Sullivans home. Left to right, front row: Mae Burns Perry, Violet Lideen, Marie O'Hearne, unidentified. Second row: Margaret McCourt, Della Murty, unidentified, Clara O'Hearn, Gladys Klock, Gertrude Sullivan. Third row: Jessie Sullivan, Murty, Mrs. Murty, Mrs. Sullivan. *Courtesy, Audrey Perry*

BUSINESS

Some of the names are still familiar, especially the family-owned DiCamillo Bakery, based on Linwood Avenue in the city's North End.

Others were part of the retail sector here for years: Mahoney's Drug Store, the Butler Grocery Store, and Max Amberg, whose descendants operated the clothing store until the 1960s.

This section of the book also reminds us of the "Little House on the Corner," the first building of Mount St. Mary's Hospital, and the Niagara Falls Memorial Hospital (later Medical Center), when it operated a nurses training school from 1897 to 1935.

And the hotels like the Cataract House, the International, and the Mount Eagle were among the finest on the Niagara Frontier.

Lobianco and Son Grocery store at 1001 Niagara Street. Included in the picture are: Sam Lobianco, Mary Lobianco and Rose Morell, 1940s. *Courtesy, Betty Lobianco*

Samuel Hirsch Dry Goods, 117 Falls Street, Niagara Falls, late 1800s. *Courtesy, Niagara County Historical Society*

James J. Mahoney Drug Store, International Block, Niagara Falls. Left to right: H.C. Burns, C. Mahony, Abe Davey. *Courtesy, Niagara County Historical Society*

William S. Humbert Cement, lime, plaster store, 144 Buffalo Avenue Niagara Falls. *Courtesy, Niagara County Historical Society*

Jim Mullane's Bar on Buffalo Avenue and 10th Street, Barney Mullane on left with canal workers. *Courtesy, Bernard Mullane*

Butler Grocery, owned by Mitchell G. Butler, Niagara Falls. *Courtesy, Niagara County Historical Society*

Wm. Robido and Morton Shop 9 West Falls Street, Niagara Falls. Wm. Robido is the first man on the left and Mr. Morton is on the far right. The man in the middle is not identified. Niagara Falls, early 1900s. *Courtesy, Niagara County Historical Society*

George H. Salt and Company, druggist and pharmacists, 104 Falls Street, Niagara Falls, late 1800s. *Courtesy, Niagara County Historical Society*

Max Amberg Clothing, 119 Falls Street, Niagara Falls. Max is on the right. Late 1800s. *Courtesy, Niagara County Historical Society*

S.D. True Company, sold oil cloth, draperies, curtains, and carpets at 108-110 Falls Street. Stephan D. True was the proprietor. The lady on the right is F.E. True and possibly the man to her left is Stephan, Niagara Falls, circa 1905. *Courtesy, Niagara County Historical Society*

American Palace Steam Laundry, 306 Main Street, Niagara Falls. W.P. Campbell agent. *Courtesy, Niagara County Historical Society*

Hotel Nassau, 112 Falls Street, Niagara Falls. H.C. Fuchs Proprietor, late 1800s. *Courtesy, Niagara County Historical Society*

Chester Schweitzer Cataract Ice Company delivery wagon, late 1800s. *Courtesy, Beatrice Hazel Cook*

Mae Burns and friend in front of the Mohn and Hunter laundry where she worked, circa 1910.
Courtesy, Audrey Perry

Chester Schweitzer Cataract Ice Company delivery truck, circa 1925. *Courtesy, Beatrice Hazel Cook*

The original site of DiCamillo Bakery located on 14th Street between Walnut and Ferry Avenue. Tom DiCamillo on right with Joe DiCamillo in center, sons of founder Thomas DiCamillo. Jim S'Dao is on the left with fleet of delivery trucks. The Bakery was located in the basement and the family grocery store was on the first floor. Photo taken in 1938. *Courtesy, DiCamillo Family*

John Irwin and Company Electrical Contractors, 2778 Main Street, Niagara Falls, late 1800s. *Courtesy, Niagara County Historical Society*

Max H. Elbe, Sr., standing in front of his jewelry store, circa 1905, Niagara Falls. *Courtesy, Niagara County Historical Society*

General Store, 3340 Niagara Falls Blvd. which is now 9534 Cayuga Drive owned by Robert William Smith, 1920. *Courtesy, Alice Smith Lasher*

Falls Restaurant, circa 1900. *Courtesy, Niagara Falls Public Library*

C.E. Grauer Shop, and Ackerman and Tierney on Main Street, Niagara Falls, circa 1900. *Courtesy, Niagara County Historical Society*

P. Lammerts Carriage painting shop, circa 1900. Peter, third from the right, was an immigrant from Denmark around 1850. *Courtesy, Jim and Jody Gra*

Woodworking shop, Lammerts Auto Works, 6th Street, circa 1920. *Courtesy, Jim and Jody Gray*

Lammerts Auto Works, machine shop on 6th Street, circa 1920. Note, power shaft, boxed in, running along ceiling just to left of center. This shaft turned belts to power tools. *Courtesy, Jim and Jody Gray*

Cashier's office, Lammerts Auto Works, circa 1920, note, radiator on shelf. *Courtesy, Jim and Jody Gray*

Lammerts Auto Works, the first Cadillac dealership in the world. Cadillacs were shipped F.O.B. from Detroit by rail. Peter Lammerts picked them up for customers and readied them for use. When several didn't pick their cars up, he contacted Cadiallic Motor Company and arranged permission to sell them himself in 1917. *Courtesy, Jim and Jody Gray*

Lammerts Cadillac, Buick, Opel newly opened, early 1960s. This was the first time in history GM allowed two makes (Cadillac and Buick) to be sold in one building. *Courtesy, Jim and Jody Gray*

Nurses in front of Mount St. Mary's Hospital, known as "The Little House on the Corner" 1907-1914, Niagara Falls. *Courtesy, Mount St. Mary's Hospital*

Founded in 1907 and known as the "Little House on the Corner", the 30 bed hospital on Sixth Street and Ferry Avenue, was the first building of Mount St. Mary's Hospital. The influx of industry into the City of Niagara Falls created a corresponding increase in population and the need for a larger hospital. So, in 1914, the second structure, a 185 bed hospital was opened on 6th Street. This building remained the hospital until February 14, 1965 when the hospital was moved to Lewiston and the building was converted into a nursing home, the present St. Mary's Manor.

St. Mary's Hospital, early 1900s. *Courtesy, Niagara Falls Public Library*

Former St. Mary's Hospital, later became St. Mary's Manor, 6th Street, 1914-1965, Niagara Falls. *Courtesy, Mount St. Mary's Hospital*

Niagara Falls Memorial Hospital (later Medical Center) operated a nurses training school from 1897-1935. More than 330 women graduaed from the school in its 38-year history. Members of the last graduating class, along with the school's director, M. Helen Gibbard, (center) posed before commencement exercises, June 11, 1935, in the auditorium of the Shredded Wheat Company building. *Courtesy, Memorial Medical Center Foundation*

Red Coach Inn, Niagara Falls, 1920s. *Courtesy, Niagara Falls Public Library*

Imperial Hotel, Niagara Falls, 1920s. *Courtesy, Niagara Falls Public Library*

Hotel Vancouver, Niagara Falls, early 1900s. *Courtesy, Niagara Falls Public Library*

Eldorado Hotel was a hub of Youngstown social life in the "Gay '90s." It was built by Frank Steele Sr., a mystery man from about 1860-1890. Many people came for a week, month or the whole summer to a lovely spot which provided comfortable rooms, delicious food and dancing to delightful music in the huge ballroom. Fort Niagara was less than a mile away and its presence certainly enhanced the social life of the village. *Courtesy, Town of Porter Historical Society*

The Barton House was built in Youngstown in the 1830s as a hotel by Alexander Barton. In 1863, a fire consumed many valuable buildings in the town, and one of these was the Barton House. *Courtesy, Town of Porter Historical Society*

Clifton Hotel, Niagara Falls, 1920s.
Courtesy, Niagara Falls Public Library

Wakemen's Hotel and Restaurant, Niagara Falls, 1930s. *Courtesy, Niagara Falls Public Library*

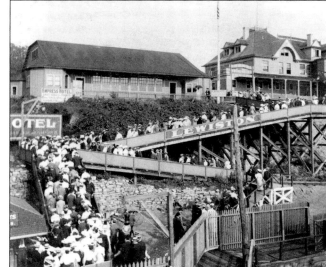

Passengers waiting to board Steamer Cayuga at what is now Riverside Inn, Lewiston.
Courtesy, Lewiston Historical Society

International Hotel, Niagara Falls, circa 1910. *Courtesy, Russell Nelson*

The Franklin House, circa 1900. *Courtesy, Audrey Perry*

Hotel Columbia, Niagara Falls. *Courtesy, Niagara Falls Public Library*

Power City Hotel, Niagara Falls. *Courtesy, Niagara Falls Public Library*

Ruby Pelton, Lilly Burns, Majorie and Rose Raines are seen on the veranda of the W.J. Raines Hotel, 1914. *Courtesy, Audrey Perry*

N.Y. Central Hotel on Depot Avenue. *Courtesy, Audrey Perry*

Mount Eagle Hotel. *Courtesy, Audrey Perry*

Interior view of the dining room at the Cataract House, circa 1890. *Courtesy, Niagara Falls Public Library*

Aerial view of the Cataract House with the Falls in the background. *Courtesy, Niagara Falls Public Library*

Cataract House fire, October, 1945. *Courtesy, Niagara Falls Public Library*

Cataract House fire, October 1945. *Courtesy, Niagara Falls Public Library*

Cataract House fire, October, 1945. *Courtesy, Niagara Falls Public Library*

Bellevue Theater, built, 1921. *Courtesy, Niagara Falls Public Library*

International Theatre, Niagara Falls. *Courtesy, Audrey Perry*

Interior of the Bellevue Theater, North Main Street. *Courtesy, Niagara Falls Public Library*

Remodeling the International Theatre next to the new Gorge Auditorium. *Courtesy, Niagara Falls Public Library*

This audience enjoys a movie at the Lumberg Theater, circa 1920s. It was closed May 1928 and razed June 1928.

Courtesy, Niagara Falls Public Library

Alfred Nicholas owner of "Al's Barber Shop" next to The Rite Spot on Old Falls Street, 1933. *Courtesy, Anthony Nicholas*

Ontario House, Youngstown, a stone building on the corner of Lockport and Main streets was built in 1842 on the site of the old Hathaway Tavern - one of the earliest taverns to do business on the Frontier in 1815. *Courtesy, Town of Porter Historical Society*

Vito Palumbo selling fruit on Willow Avenue, circa 1920. *Courtesy Tom Palumbo*

Amin M. Touma standing in his new store, Touma's Confectionary and Ice Cream Parlor at 50 Falls Street, Niagara Falls, 1905. *Courtesy, Richard A. Touma*

Touma's Confectionary and Ice Cream Parlor, 1905-1958, 50 Falls Street, Niagara Falls, photo, 1958. *Courtesy, Richard A. Touma*

Touma's Confectionary and Ice Cream Parlor at 50 Falls Street, Niagara Falls, 1958. *Courtesy, Richard A. Touma*

Touma's Confectionary and Ice Cream Parlor at 50 Falls Street, Niagara Falls, 1958. *Courtesy, Richard A. Touma*

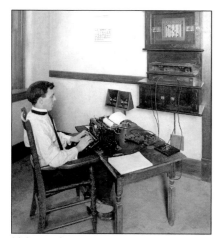

Telegraph operators room, *Niagara Gazette*, early March, 1915. *Courtesy, Niagara Falls Public Library*

Stenotyping room, *Niagara Gazette*, early March, 1915. *Courtesy, Niagara Falls Public Library*

Exterior of the *Niagara Gazette*, March, 1915. *Courtesy, Niagara Falls Public Library*

City news room at the *Niagara Gazette*, March, 1915. *Courtesy, Niagara Falls Public Library*

Niagara Gazette delivery truck, a 1914 Model T. *Courtesy, Niagara Falls Public Library*

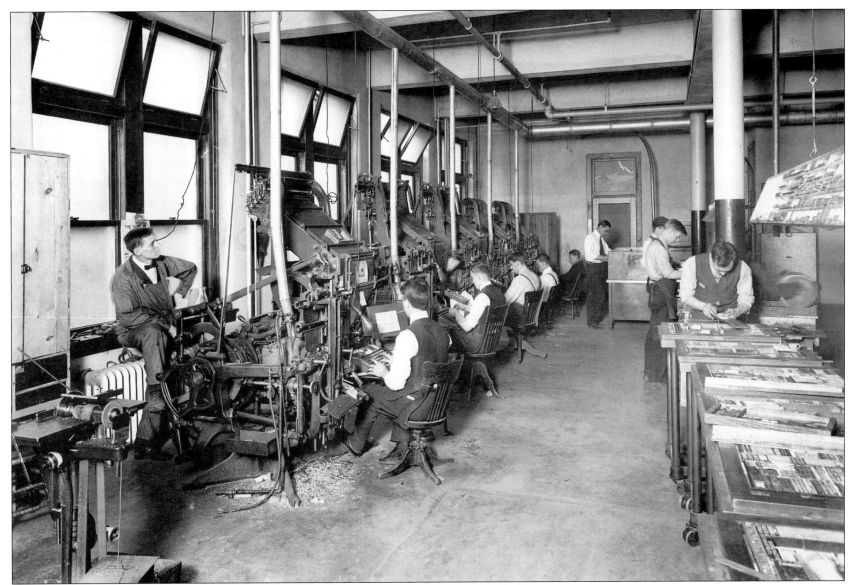

Linotype room at the *Niagara Gazette*, March, 1915. *Courtesy, Niagara Falls Public Library*

Socony's service station at the corner of Pine Avenue and 56th Street, circa 1929. *Courtesy, Geraldine Biehl Tracey*

Cooper Sign Company in the 1920s located on Mang Avenue in the village of LaSalle, now located at 7350 Porter Road, Town of Niagara. *Courtesy, Cooper Sign Company*

Fratello Bros. Groceries and Meats. C. Cosmo Fratello and his son, Charles, behind counter, Anthone, and Salvatore, pose for this photo, circa 1930. The store was located at 128 Memorial Parkway. The store was founded by Mr. Fratello and was in operation from 1920 to 1947, when they relocated to 3010 Pine Avenue. Fratello Bros. were noted for their delicious Italian sausage. The family sold the business in 1961, and it is now the site of Scipiones Catering. *Courtesy, Charlotte Tompkins*

Paul E. Maloney's Gas station on River Road, LaSalle, 1926. One year later, River Road was renamed Buffalo Avenue. The building has had several additions and this original portion is the present office of Richardson Auto Repair at 8652 Buffalo Avenue. *Courtesy, Roy Richardson*

Henry Merlin on left and Mr. Robinson on right, in front of Robinson's Garage, circa 1930. *Courtesy, Jeff Merlin*

Haskell Store, Youngstown, was built in 1855 by the well known brick builder, John Carter. It was built for the founder B.D. Davis. The store was originally divided into two sections; one for groceries and the other for general merchandise. *Courtesy, Town of Porter Historical Society*

T. Trapasso 1823 Pine Avenue, near City Market, 1947. *Courtesy Tom Palumbo*

Employees of Jenss Brothers Department store gathered for this picture before they departed for the annual picnic at Olcott Beach, 1937. The founder of the store was Frank A. Jenss, mayor of the city in 1932. Vice-president J. Gordon Jenss is seen reclining on the pavement. *Courtesy, Ms. Janelle Jenss Montazzoli*

Lunch counter, S.S. Kresge Company, Falls Street. Photo is for the store anniversary. *Courtesy, Josephine Cirrito*

Hachee's Gas station on the northwest corner of Niagara Falls Blvd. and Tuscarora Road, 1940. *Courtesy Roy Richardson*

Giant Food Market picnic, 1938. Nick Meranto was the owner and Al Whitehead was the manager. *Courtesy, A. John Paradise*

The Real Spot on Main Street, Fred Aquino was the owner, early 1940s. *Courtesy, Rose Marie DeMarco Aquino*

Louis Restaurant fire, Niagara Falls, June 1967. *Courtesy, Samuel M. Golden*

Prospect Street, looking east, Hancock Building and United Building. Downtown Niagara Falls, part of Urban Renewal, June 1969. *Courtesy, Samuel M. Golden*

Al Frosolone serving ice cream at Frosolones General Store, 2706 Highland Avenue, 1953. *Courtesy, Alfred Frosolone*

INDUSTRY

iagara's industrial strength was shaped by the hydropower era. In June 1956, a dramatic event changed the course of the city, with nearly 25 percent of the tax base wiped out by the collapse of the Schoellkopf Power Station into the Niagara Gorge.

While the city has lost thousands of manufacturing jobs in the past few decades, it once could claim the title, "Electrochemical Capital of the World."

One of its most famous plants was "The Home of Shredded Wheat," which offered tours for visitors from around the world. After viewing the various operations at the spotless facility on Buffalo Avenue, the visitors were invited to the cafeteria for a bowl of shredded wheat, topped with fresh fruit from Niagara County.

Robert Moses Power Plant, September, 1960. *Courtesy, Samuel M. Golden*

It is believed that these men are employees of the Niagara Falls Power House, 1880s. *Courtesy, Marlene Beazley*

One of the first Niagara Falls Power Company service wagons. *Courtesy, Niagara Falls Public Library*

Factories atop the high bank. After the water from the hydraulic canal was used for powering the factories, it was allowed to flow back into the river, 1895. *Courtesy, Niagara County Historical Society*

Early 1900s Niagara Gorge lined with power plants. *Courtesy, Barbara Willick*

Collapse of Schoellkopf Power Station, June 1956. *Courtesy, Niagara Falls Public Library*

Schoellkopf Power Company station collapse, June 1956. *Courtesy, Niagara Falls Public Library*

Schoellkopf Power Station fell in the gorge, June 1956. *Courtesy, Niagara Falls Public Library*

Edmund Dean Adams Power Station on Buffalo Avenue, Niagara Falls, 1941.
Courtesy, Niagara County Historical Society

Dedication of Power Portal Arch, June 13, 1967 on Goat Island. Governor Nelson A. Rockefeller and Joseph J. Metro shaking hands. *Courtesy, Joseph Metro*

Niagara Power Plant Project N5 view looking down and west at 84" Royal Avenue Sewer over conduit November 1, 1960. *Courtesy, Paul D. Kaczmarzyk*

Niagara Power Project-contract N5 view looking northwest showing backfill operation of manhole at west side of Royal Avenue, 1960. *Courtesy, Paul D. Kaczmarzyk*

Niagara Power Project contract N5 view looking west northwest at Parkway progress with industrial intake and dock street bridge in foreground with intakes and cofferdam in background, 1960. *Courtesy, Paul D. Kaczmarzyk*

Niagara Power Project N5 view looking east at form work for connecting tunnel November 1, 1960. *Courtesy, Paul D. Kaczmarzyk*

Carborundum Cadet Corp, October 1916. Prior to the entrance of the United States into World War I, extensive preparations were made throughout the country in the event the country should be drawn in. Carborundum organized the Cadet Corps under the leadership of Charles G. Campbell and Frederick W. Gray, Lieutenant. Uniforms were supplied and wooden guns for drills: drills were held weekly with no loss of time to the employees. Many of these men served in World War I and earned commissions early because of the instruction received in this Cadet Corps. *Courtesy, Niagara Falls Public Library*

Carborundum main office staff, September 1915. Notice the absence of women in this group. There were no women on the office staff until the time of the first World War. *Courtesy, Niagara Falls Public Library*

Miss Kay Morrow surrounded by many thousands of fan letters in response to Carborundum Band Radio program for one week. All of these letters requested a souvenir stone promised if writing in. This plan was discontinued soon after and later the radio program was also discontinued, photo circa 1929. *Courtesy, Niagara Falls Public Library*

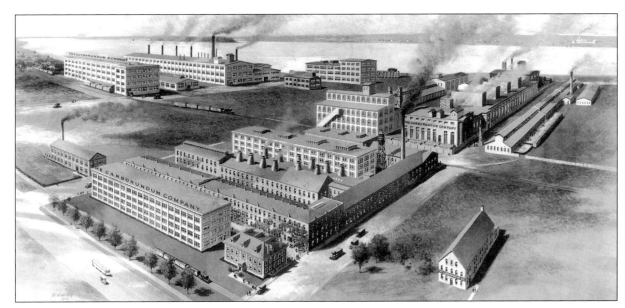

Carborundum Company plant.
Courtesy, Niagara Falls Public Library

Carborundum Company plant,
circa 1895. *Courtesy, Niagara Falls*
Public Library

Oldbury Corporation workers, 1933. Henry Merlin is on top. *Courtesy, Jeff Merlin*

Eary view of Nabisco, "The Home of Shredded Wheat." Showing the beauty of its location, fronting a park on the Company's property adjoining the upper Niagara River. *Courtesy, Niagara Falls Public Library*

Hooker Chemical Company on Buffalo Avenue, circa 1965. *Courtesy, Niagara Falls Public Library*

Shredded Wheat wagons distributed Shredded Wheat samples house-to-house.

Courtesy, Niagara Falls Public Library

Women packing shredded wheat. *Courtesy, Niagara Falls Public Library*

Visitors were served breakfast at the Shredded Wheat Company. *Courtesy, Niagara Falls Public Library*

SCHOOLS & EDUCATION

Many of the schools featured in this section are no longer in existence.

But the photos of the buildings and the people provide a glimpse of those unforgettable days at Center Avenue School, Sugar Street (Hyde Park Boulevard) School, and the Red Brick School on Lockport Street in Youngstown, to name a few.

There's even an overview of the DeVeaux School campus (1965), soon to become part of the New York state parks system.

Maple Avenue School, fourth grade, 1950. *Courtesy, Barbara Willick*

Third Street School students, circa 1895. *Courtesy, Audrey Perry*

First Third Street School, built 1857, taken down, 1897. *Courtesy, Niagara Falls Public Library*

Cleveland Avenue School. *Courtesy, Niagara Falls Public Library*

Cleveland Avenue School class, fourth grade, 1947-48. *Courtesy Fredericek R. Fields*

Cleveland Avenue School students, 1897. *Courtesy, Niagara Falls Public Library*

Sixth grade class, 1929, 17th Street School. *Courtesy, A. John Paradise*

Lewiston Academy. *Courtesy, Niagara Falls Public Library*

Center Avenue School, circa 1920. *Courtesy, Alfred Frosolone*

Old Lewiston Academy, Lewiston, burned in the early 1900s. *Courtesy, Lewiston Historical Society*

Sugar Street School, built 1895. *Courtesy, Niagara Falls Public Library*

Niagara Falls High School was built in 1902, and burned in 1922. *Courtesy, Niagara Falls Public Library*

Sugar Creek School class, located on Hyde Park near "C" Street, circa 1903. *Courtesy, Geraldine Biehl Tracey*

Niagara Falls High School after the January 1922 fire. *Courtesy, Niagara Falls Public Library*

Trott Vocational High School. *Courtesy, Niagara Falls Public Library*

Kindergarden class Niagara Street School, 1938. *Courtesy, Beatrice Hazel Cook*

Trott Vocational High School, football team, circa 1937. *Courtesy, Tom Palumbo*

The Red Brick School on Lockport Street in Youngstown was originally four rooms. It was built in 1892 for $8,000. It was enlarged in 1922 and 1927. *Courtesy, Town of Porter Historical Society*

Kindergarden class 66th Street School, 1955. Mrs, Eddy was the teacher. *Courtesy, Niagara Falls Public Library*

Evershed Elementary School, fifth grade class, Ruth Maxwell was the teacher. The school was located on 56th Street, circa 1936. *Courtesy, Geraldine Biehl Tracey*

St. Theresa School, seventh grade, 1953. *Courtesy, Barbara Willick*

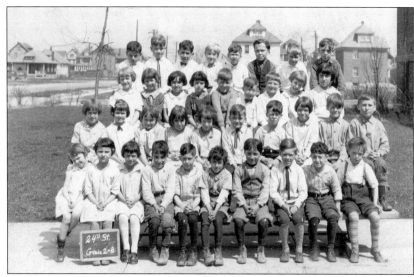

24th Street School, second grade photo, early 1930s. *Courtesy Edward Wysocki*

The play, "Band Wagon" cast North Junior High School, May, 1952. *Courtesy, Mark Johnston*

Maple Avenue School, first grade, 1946. *Courtesy, Barbara Willick*

Aerial view of the DeVeaux School campus, circa 1965. *Courtesy, Donald E. Loker, DeVeaux Archivist*

Ground breaking in 1929 for an extension on the old gymnasium which dated from 1869, DeVeaux School. *Courtesy, Donald E. Loker, DeVeaux Archivist*

The DeVeaux School cooks preparing a meal in the kitchen, Spring of 1953. Left to right: Miss Benny Tolin and Mrs. Rosa Ward. *Courtesy, Donald E. Loker, DeVeaux Archivist*

Laying the Cornerstone for Schoellkopf Hall, the new dormitory for boys, DeVeaux School, November 3, 1929. Left to right: Reverend Dr. William S. Barrows, Headmaster, Reverend Doctor Cameron Davis, Class of 1890, Mr. Paul Schoellkopf who donated $50,000 for construction of the building, Paul Schoellkopf, Jr., his son, and Rt. Reverend Frederic L. Deans, a Bishop from Scotland. *Courtesy, Donald E. Loker, DeVeaux Archivist*

St. Vincent's Hall, Niagara University. *Courtesy, Niagara Falls Public Library*

Niagara University, Sister's Convent, built 1909. *Courtesy, Niagara Falls Public Library*

Alumni Hall, Niagara University. *Courtesy, Niagara Falls Public Library*

Alumni Hall, Niagara University, was destroyed by fire, March 14, 1913. *Courtesy, Niagara Falls Public Library*

PEOPLE

Niagara Falls is a community that prides itself on diversity. From its earliest days -- before the Village of Suspension Bridge and the Town of Niagara from the municipality in 1892 -- there was always a strong work ethic in Niagara, whether small shops along the North End or in the smokestack industries along Buffalo Avenue.

After the Erie Canal was built there was a steady influx of new residents to upstate areas. In the Niagara area, many of the immigrants, after arriving in New York or Boston found their way to the Niagara Frontier.

Clinging to old world habits and their ties to families and friends who came before them, many of the new residents -- Irish, Italian and Poles tended to settle into their own neighborhoods.

During World War II, a number of African-Americans came up from the South to work in the industries here. Niagara, an international tourist destination and a place to call home.

The Chormann sisters taken pre-1908 at a 50th Anniversary party. *Courtesy, Alice Smith Lasher*

Victor and Ann Dickson at their Silver Anniversary, 1968. *Courtesy, Eugene Dickson*

Neighborhood kids at Maple Avenue off Hyde Park Blvd., 1943. *Courtesy, Barbara Willick*

Anna and Andrew Willick. *Courtesy, Barbara Willick*

Gerald Dorgan on Falls Street, 1930s. *Courtesy, Eugene Dickson*

Jack Lemon, Mayor Lackey and Councilman Pat Dillon with Iney Wallens when a movie was made in Niagara Falls, 1968. Mrs Wallens was president of Operation Petticoat Progress. *Courtesy, Iney Wallens*

Dorothy Willick at the falls, 1936. *Courtesy, Barbara Willick*

Evelyn, James, Dorothy, and Jenny Steer at Porter Park, Quay Street and Buffalo Avenue. *Courtesy, Barbara Willick*

James Henry Meehan, 1869, was the first Niagara Falls resident to win a scholarship to Cornell.

Courtesy, Marlene Beazley

Mary Meehan Robertson at the Falls, 1920s. *Courtesy, Marlene Beazley*

Stanley and his son Theodore Golda, Niagara Falls, 1929. *Courtesy Theodore Golda*

Jean Dojka and Larry Keller wearing their new Easter outfits, 1932. *Courtesy, Jean Dojka*

Jacob Pasek wearing home guide society uniform in front of Holy Trinity Church. He was one of the founders of the church, 1912. *Courtesy, Jean Dojka*

Jenny Oliwiecki saw Mary Pickford in a movie eight times so she could copy and sew her outfit, the hat, dress, purse, gloves and decorate her shoes. Circa 1924. *Courtesy, Jean Dojka*

Gail Daggett, Dottie Braden and Jeannie Rice pose for this photo at souvenir booth on Falls Street, circa 1937.

Courtesy, Jeanne Rice Phelps

Emelia Keller and son Anthony J. Keller, 1908. *Courtesy Jean Dojka*

Alice Smith over log bridge at 96th Street and Cayuga Drive, 1930. *Courtesy, Alice Smith Lasher*

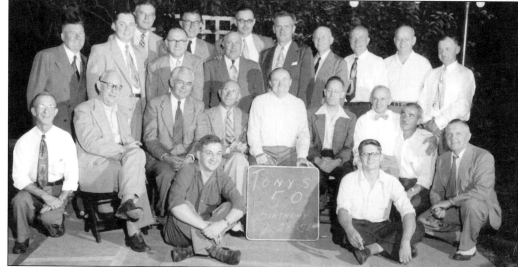

Tony Keller 50th birthday party, 1951. Left to right, sitting, front row: Edwin S. Dojka, Larry Keller. Second row: Stephen Pinkowski, Dr. Leo Rozan, R. Bugay, Ben Kaszyca, Anthony J. Keller, Henry Zimmer, Joe Mady, Anthony Zabkowski, Mr. Lasota. Third row: Anthony Zabkowski, Richard Niewiadomski, Mr. Kaszyca, Mr. Chiarenza,, Mr. Gniazdowski, Felix Stempien, Mr. Bienek, Mr. Stempien, Z. Dojka. Fourth row: Joe Lach, J. Szelest, Stanley Jarosz. *Courtesy Jean Dojka*

Mrs. Mary Nassoiy, 1045 Cleveland Avenue. *Courtesy, Audrey Perry*

John Domenic Nassoiy at 1045 Cleveland Avenue. *Courtesy, Audrey Perry*

The Michael and Clarissa (Nassoiy) Perry family, shortly after they moved to Niagara Falls in 1893. From left to right: Ida Perry, Clarissa holding Agnes Perry, Henry Perry, Eugene Perry, Michael and Loretto Perry. *Courtesy, Audrey Perry*

Lillian Hickox Burns with her son, Harry and daughter Rose Estell, 1880s. *Courtesy, Audrey Perry*

Vine Harrington Hickox, seated, is flanked by his children, Charles, Lillian Esther and Anna Mae, 1880s. *Courtesy, Audrey Perry*

Mae Burns and Ed Ruhlman, 1920. *Courtesy, Audrey Perry*

Majorie Raines, three months, 1902. *Courtesy, Audrey Perry*

Art Deluca on right and Ed Darin on left, 1944.
Courtesy, Jeff Merlin

Geraldine Merlin wearing riding outfit, 1941. *Courtesy, Jeff Merlin*

Henry Merlin on the right and John Ricco on left, 1937. *Courtesy, Jeff Merlin*

Henry Merlin on left and John Ricco on right, 1936. *Courtesy, Jeff Merlin*

Greg Olsen, Mark and Bonnie Johnston at 3735 McKoon Avenue selling lemonade, 1967. *Courtesy, Mark Johnston*

Bonnie Johnston and Mike Skurski selling lemonade. *Courtesy, Mark Johnston*

Wedding Day, Monsora and Amin M. Touma, October 7, 1915. *Courtesy, Richard A. Touma*

Helen Touma and her mother Monsora, 1936. *Courtesy, Richard A. Touma*

Richard Touma and cousin Lila in front of store, 1957. *Courtesy, Richard A. Touma*

Monsora Touma behind soda fountain, 1955. *Courtesy, Richard A. Touma*

Amin Touma and son, Richard across the street from store in Prospect Park, 1938. *Courtesy, Richard A. Touma*

Mike Mendola
and Tom Mendola
on 20th Street,
early 1940s.
Courtesy, Mike Mendola

Gregory and Roz Mendola, circa
1940. *Courtesy, Mike Mendola*

This family stand in front of the the first home torn down
during the Love Canal Cleanup, 99th and Frontier Avenue.
Left to right: George Greenwald, Lewis Greenwald, Lydie
Greenwald, Alfred Mason, Margaret Greenwald Mason, Maude
Mason, Joseph Mason, Barbara Chormann Greenwald, Robert
Smith, Susan Greenwald Smith, 1890s. *Courtesy, Alice Smith Lasher*

Friends at the Alps Restaurant. Gregory Mendola, Geroge
Churakos, and other friends, 1957. *Courtesy, Mike Mendola*

Mike Mendola, Ron DeLuke, Paul Smith and Doug
Pike at 318 8th Street. *Courtesy, Mike Mendola*

Susanna Gruenvaldt Smith, circa
1910. *Courtesy, Alice Smith Lasher*

Navy Club of the United States of America Auxiliary, 1952. *Courtesy, Alice Smith Lasher*

Birthday party, 51st for Rita Smith at the Executive dining room, 1943. *Courtesy, Alice Smith Lasher*

Four generations. From right: Susanna Smith, Robert William Smith holding Robert Lee Lasher and Alice Smith Lasher. *Courtesy, Alice Smith Lasher*

Rose Marie DeMarco Aquino, February 10, 1946 in front of DeMarco's Grocery, 13th between East Falls Street and Buffalo Avenue. *Courtesy, Mary Grace DeMarco Monaco*

DeMarco and Colosi children and friends in front of DeMarco's Grocery 13th Street between East Falls and Buffalo Avenue. *Courtesy, Mary Grace DeMarco Monaco*

Cliff Collins in front of MacDonald Florist, 1951. *Courtesy, Cliff Collins*

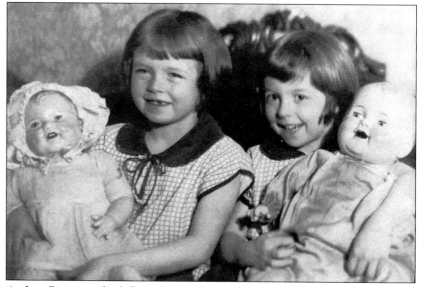

50th Anniversary, December 15, 1950 of Tomaso and Maria Rose Trapasso with family. From left: Joe and Grace Trapasso, Dan Palumbo, Al and Ann Trapasso, Joan Trapasso, Dom and Peggy Pulano, Anthony, Mabel and Beverly Trapasso, Frank and Emma Trapasso. Seated: Marie Palumbo, Rose Trapasso, Tumaso & Maria Rose Trapasso, Sam and Clara Trapasso. Kneeling: Tommy Trapasso, Don Trapasso, Sharon Trapasso, Janice Palumbo, Tom Palumbo.

Audrey Perry on the left and sister Rheta Perry Melcher, circa 1930. *Courtesy, Audrey Perry*

RECREATION & CELEBRATION

Niagara's always afforded splendid recreational opportunities. Aside from professional sports including minor league baseball franchises over the years our community has provided excellent recreational facilities for citizens of all ages.

Many longtime residents remember baseball pitcher Sal (the Barber) Maglie, who starred with the New York Giants and later the Brooklyn Dodgers in the 1950's.

But, on the home front, Niagara had some outstanding successes too, with its popular industrial baseball leagues, a hockey team from LaSalle winning the Western New York championship in 1920-21, and the Niagara Drag Strip in the Town of Niagara.

The community was quick to celebrate too, whether it was the end of the war or pageantry at Old Fort Niagara. Even the King and Queen of England found their way to Niagara Falls, New York in 1939, when the cornerstone was laid for a new international bridge over the Niagara Gorge.

Niagara Falls' bicycle club, circa 1895. *Courtesy, Niagara Falls Public Library*

This group of men were from the local bicycle club in the 1890s. From left to right, William Campbell, Neil Campbell, George G. Shepard, Hector MacBean, Felix Woolworth. *Courtesy, Niagara Falls Public Library*

International Paper Company, municipal league baseball champions, Niagara Falls, 1929. *Courtesy, Niagara Falls Public Library*

Niagara Falls High School basketball team, 1915-1916. *Courtesy, Niagara Falls Public Library*

Stars and Stripes track team, 1906-1907. Mickey Considine, Frank Long, Ernie Green, Bill O'Hair, Dan Reilly, Grant Moyer, Yellow Fitch. Manager was Geo. Nolan. *Courtesy, Niagara Falls Public Library*

Hockey championships of Western New York, 1920-21. Left to right, back row: Arthur Hartley, Harold Greenwald, Harry Pack, Ted Hilderbrandt, Raymond Mang, Ben Hilderbrandt. Front row: Tony Hilderbrandt, Elmer Luick, Edward Gross, Art Kinghorn, William Stone. *Courtesy, Alice Smith Lasher*

Ted Szpara at Niagara Drag Strip, 1969. *Courtesy, Ted Szpara*

Ted Szpara, Don Ames and Karl Blair, Niagara Drag Strip, 1969. *Courtesy, Ted Szpara*

Henry Merlin with homemade racing car "Spirit of Niagara Falls," 1932. *Courtesy, Jeff Merlin*

Lydia and Lloyd Fox, Maggie and Joe Mason in a canoe on Black Creek at Bergholtz Creek, 1890s. *Courtesy, Alice Smith Lasher*

These young men were players on a base-ball team called Clifton Clowns during the 1940s. The Clifton Hotel housed the popular night club called the Jade Room. From left to right: unknown, Jack Fitzgerald (in back) Bob Owen, owner of the hotel, and Bob Davis. *Courtesy, Hazel Davis*

Gregory Mendola and friends at Central Bowling Lanes on 19th Street, late 1940s. *Courtesy, Mike Mendola*

The parade gounds of Old Fort Niagara in 1934 during a day of celebration for the completion of the fort's restoration. *Courtesy, Old Fort Niagara Association*

A group of the Niagara Falls Service League dancers rests a moment between rehearsals for the Masque of the Pageant Drama of Old Fort Niagara, nightly feature of the Four-Nation Celebration at Niagara, September 3-6, 1934. The group consists of Marjorie Koethen, Millicent Arthurs, Mary Benner, Mary Lou McDonald, Margaret McDonald, Jeanne MacDonald, Hilda Douglas, Sally Knauff, Mrs. Ralph House, Beth Freel, Anna Swanoe, Mrs. Emily Klaussen, Mrs. Calvin N. Knauff, Trudy Lansing and Esther Elderfield. *Courtesy, Old Fort Niagara Association*

Carborundum office employees participating in Preparedness Parade, 1916. Front row, left to right: F.D. Bowman, C.E. Hawke, F.I. Pierce, G.R. Rayner and F.W. Gray. *Courtesy, Niagara Falls Public Library*

A parade celebrating the return of Company E from the war, 1919. *Courtesy, Audrey Perry*

Parade passing Payne's Floor Coverings on East Falls Street, early 1960s. *Courtesy Fredericek R. Fields*

Parade on Main Street, now the site of Earl Brydges Library, 1960s. *Frederick R. Fields*

King and Queen of England visit Niagara, 1939. *Courtesy, Alfred Frosolone*

First Pride and Progress parade held in Niagara Falls in May of 1963. Members of "Operation Petticoat Progress" kick off the first week with a picnic and parade. This was a civic organization that worked closely with Mayor Lackey to beautify and uplift the spirit of Niagara. Iney Wallens, president of this organization is on the far right of the float.

Courtesy, Iney Wallens

Christmas display, December 1959, sponsored by the Catholic War Veterans. *Courtesy, Samuel M. Golden*

An art festival at the old Lewiston library on Center Street, Lewiston. *Courtesy, Samuel M. Golden*